Basketball Head

Tips and tricks on Becoming a Successful Student-Athlete

D1565544

I would like to thank my mom for always pushing me to be better, my dad for keeping my mind peaceful and helping me relieve stress and my stepfather for driving me to a lot of practices and games.

Three coaches that have had a major impact on my life: Coach Knox for always pushing me beyond my skill level, knowing what I was capable of on and off the court. Coach Johnny Cooper and Coach Jessie for helping bring out my leadership abilities and team skills.

Ms. Current for always letting me know that teaching goes beyond the classroom.

My best friend Lauren for always being there for me on and off the court even while living overseas.

Team Fly AAU Girls' basketball team and coaches for giving me my first AAU experience and one of the best.

To all my family and friends, whether you took me to practice, cheered me on at a game, or brought me a pair of sneakers for the season.

Thank You from the bottom of my heart.

Introduction

I came up with the idea to write this book because a couple of years ago my mother and I were in a bookstore and I was looking for a book similar to the one that I am writing and I could not find anything. So my mother said to me why you don't write a book for young people from your perspective. I thought she was crazy. I was like who would want to read something that I would write, and she replied the same boy or girl that will come in here looking for the same type of book that you are looking for. I could see in my mother's eyes that she was already sold on me writing the book so I agreed. My mother, father, and I went back and forth about what the book should be about. Although I love sports, I'm also concerned about keeping my grades up so I decided to write Basketball Head for young aspiring student-athletes just like myself. I hope that everyone that reads this book finds something that they can use in their future.

Basketball Head- Tips and tricks on becoming a successful student-athlete

- My definition of a successful student-athlete is someone who loves to play sports but is also a role model for his or her peers and an academic scholar. I started playing sports at a young age. I began taking an interest in sports since the early age of two years old. I have played several sports such as basketball, soccer, tennis, track and field, and golf, but my passion is for the game of basketball. Although soccer was the first sport that I played, and I was pretty good at it. From time to time I still enjoy playing the game, but basketball has my heart. I know a lot of people may read this book and say what this child could possibly tell me about basketball.

I am just sharing with other student-athletes tips and tricks that have helped me along the way. Being a student and an athlete is something that you have to work very hard towards daily. It's not an easy task to take lightly. Webster defines a student as a *"scholar, learner, and an athlete as a person who is trained or skilled in exercises, sports, or games requiring physical strength, agility, and stamina."* So to be a student-athlete you have to be a student who is trained or skilled in exercises, sports, or games requiring physical strength, agility, and stamina. This type of title requires a lot of discipline and sacrifice from one. A lot of people like having the title of one, either a scholar or an athlete, but few dare to ride the student-athlete ride to the very end. Why? Because it's not an easy sacrifice, but it's very rewarding.

Sports

Sports date back as early 2000bc. Sports are athletic activities that involve some degree of competition. Sports are played all over the world. Every country has a sport that they are known for: In these countries particularly these sports are popular. In Europe you have soccer, In India, their sport is cricket, in Africa, they love football, in Japan, they are known for good baseball, in America you have basketball and the list goes on and on. As I stated earlier I've played several sports throughout my young life.

There is no such thing as you can only play one sport. I would suggest playing all sports that you are comfortable playing until you find one that you like. You don't have to only play one sport. You can play as many sports as you want or just the opposite. You don't have to play all sports, you can play the sport that you love the most. If sports aren't your thing, find something that is.

Typically when you are young you will play multiple sports, but as you get older you may want to focus your energy on one sport per season or just one sport. Some sports can help you get better with other sports, while other sports can affect your ability to play other sports.

There are different levels of playing sports. You have the fundamental stage where you are just learning the basics. The novices level where you are just playing for fun. On the recreational level, the sports began to be a little more organized and the rules of the different games come more into play. Recreational sports require little to no experience. Then you get into your school sports which are organized sports and consist of two levels Junior Varsity and Varsity. Typically the more skilled and advanced players will be on the Varsity team. After high school, you then have a collegiate level. You can play for a Division I, II, and III. Some schools offer club sports and intramural sports as well. After college if lucky you can play for a professional league. The good thing about sports is that there are four different seasons to play different sports. You have sports that you can play in the fall, you have sports you can play in the winter, spring, and the summer. You have sports that you can play all year long. You have some people that just play for recreation and some people that do it for their competitive nature. Some people also play the game of basketball because it is life for them, it's the outlet that they need to survive. That is how I feel about basketball it is just one of those things that keep my heart pumping. If you have a disability, don't be discouraged there are sports that you can play as well. Adaptive sports are competitive and recreational sports for people with disabilities.

I like to play multiple sports, so I can stay in shape for the next season. As I am getting ready to enter into my freshman year of high school. I am scaling back a little bit and focusing more on basketball because that is not only where my heart is but I also want to make a career out of the game.

One thing as a student-athlete you have to be careful not to exhaust yourself. You don't want to burn yourself out to the point where you are not able to give your best self to any sport. Know your limit. When your body says that it has had enough, believe it.

I remember practicing and working out for 3 hours a day 6 days a week at a very young age because I wanted to be the 1st sixth grader to make Varsity in history at my old school, Salisbury Academy. I was barely eating so I ended up crashing harder than a car on Grand Theft Auto. I was burning more calories than I was putting in. I was so dehydrated. On top of that, I was not getting the proper amount of sleep. To be a successful athlete it is important to make sure that you are in tip-top shape. To get both a quality education and to also excel at the sport that you are playing.

Bonus Activity
Need a stress reliever. Color the pictures of me to take your mind off of something.

The goal of sports

When showing interest in a sport you want to make sure that you do proper research on the sport to make sure that it is the sport for you. Below I have outlined some different sports and the goals of the sports. Just because you play the sport on a video game does not necessarily mean you know how to play the sport.

The goal of basketball is to make shots into the basket to score points. You have 5 players from each team playing on a basketball court for a total of 32 minutes. It is broken down in four 8 minutes quarters for youth, but for professionals, the quarters are normally 12 minutes long.

The goal of soccer is to move the ball down the field into the opponent's goal. Each team puts 11 players out on the field and sub them in and out during a time limit of 90 minutes broken in half to 45-minute halves.

The goal of baseball is to score points by completing more runs than the other team. There are 9 players on the field. The games last 9 innings, an inning is 2 halves and in each half one team bats until 3 outs are made while the other team tries to get a player from the other team out. An average baseball game lasts about 3 hours.

Softball is the same as baseball except it's for girls and the objective is to hit the ball before the other teams run to all four bases. The game has seven innings, but they allow anything between 3 and 7. The big difference between softball and baseball is the type of pitching. In softball, the pitch is an underhand throw and in baseball, it's an overhand throw or sidearm. The ball in softball also is a little bigger.

The goal of volleyball is to hit the ball over the net to the ground on the opponent's side. There are 6 people on the court for each team and an average game takes 90 minutes. To win the game the team has to win 3 games.

The first team to 3 games is the winner of the game. I must admit this is one of the sports that my mother could never get me to try. Not because I did not like the game but because I did not want to wear the uniform. I am very reserved about the type of clothing that I put on my body and although they have more options when it comes to volleyball uniforms I just did not want to wear anything short or clinging. Also, this is just my preference, plenty of my friends play volleyball and love it.

The goal of track and field all depends on the category that you are playing in. You can be a jumper, thrower, or runner. Jumping the longest and highest, throwing the farthest, and/or running the fastest.

Activity 1
Research a sport that you have never heard or thought to play and write down 10 reasons why you would or wouldn't play that sport.

There are different events people have to participate in and you might have to wait for those events to be over before its time for your event or you may be one of the lucky ones that event is in the beginning. The amount of participants varies as well.

I remember my first meeting like it was yesterday. My mother was so unprepared she had on heels, no shades, no snack, nothing. I was there from 6 a.m. to 8 p.m. I think she fell asleep way before me that night. The next time I had a meet she got with some of the other moms and they had a tent that had enough items for a she-shed.

The goal of tennis is to use a racket to hit the ball over the net to your opponent's side. A tennis meet can last up to 5 hours. It has 5 sets which have 3 matches in each one. With tennis, you can compete in a singles match, or two pairs in a doubles match. The player that wins the majority sets wins the game.

The goal of golf is to use a club to hit the ball into the hole with a certain amount of tees. Golf is a very long sport. You either play 9 or 18 holes depending on your level of the sport.

The goal of hockey is to shoot the puck into the goal on ice using a hockey stick. You will have 6 players on the ice, 5 skaters and 1 goaltender. Each NHL game is about 60 minutes. The game contains three 20 minute periods. During that time, the teams go back and forth trying to score the puck into the goal.

The goal of wrestling is to pin down your opponent with a takedown. A wrestling match consists of 3 periods of 4.5 minutes at middle school, and 6 in high school.

Of course, I did not cover every sport out there, but I just wanted to give you some basic knowledge of some of the most popular sports. If there is a sport that I did not cover that you want to learn about feel free to research that sport or ask a local coach about it.

Healthy Student-Athlete

It does not matter what age you are, if you plan on playing sports it is important to get a physical. Whether you are three or twenty-two, thorough physicals are important. Don't go to a doctor that is not going to do a thorough check-up because your life may depend on it. You also may want to maintain a healthy diet and exercise habits as a student-athlete. Exercise is one of the most powerful tools for anyone to improve their health and athletic abilities. Exercise can also help with your memory and help enhance learning and thinking. Nutrition is a very important piece for student-athletes as well. Good eating habits are essential because as a student-athlete you need to be able to perform both in the classroom and in the games that you will play. Your source of energy will come from the food that you are taking in. You need foods that will give you good energy, not just quick energy.

I know that as a young student-athlete the last thing that we want to worry about is the food that we are eating. You've heard this saying a million times you are what you eat.

Here is a sample of one of the weekly menu I eat, I am not saying that you should eat this. As you know there is so much that you have to factor in when it comes to your body's nutrition: weight, height, genetics, and illnesses. Consult with a doctor before making any adjustments to your eating habits. The menu that I have below is not some type of diet menu. There are plenty of other healthy options in my opinions for student-athletes but with my height and weight and the way I burn off calories, this is just a glimpse of what my weekly eating habits look like.

Monday: Breakfast- Eggs bacon grits

Snack- Fruit and Yogurt

Lunch-Ham and cheese sandwich

Snack-Popcorn

Dinner- Shrimp Alfredo

Tuesday: Breakfast- Oatmeal and toast

Snack- Oranges

Lunch- Grilled cheese

Snack-chips and salsa

Dinner- Smoked Ribs, macaroni, green beans

Wednesday: Breakfast- Pancakes and bacon

Snack- Cut up apples

Lunch- Salad

Snack-Whatever

Dinner- Chicken parmesan

Thursday: Breakfast- Sausage and egg burrito

Snack- Fruit bowl

Lunch- Chef Salad

Snack- Peanut Butter Crackers

Dinner- Lemon Pepper Salmon with Broccoli

Friday: Breakfast-Cheese Omelet

Snack- Applesauce

Lunch- Chicken salad

Snack- Peanut Butter Crackers

Dinner- Shrimp and Grits

Saturday and Sunday: Cheat Day

I am 5′ 7 and I weigh 123 pounds so my calorie intake for the day should be between 2,400 to 2,600 a day. Sometimes I go over and sometimes I am under, but I try to make sure that I exercise every day whether it's 30 minutes or 3 hours. It also helps that I have a chef in the family, so I don't get to eat out as much as I would like too. We also don't do a lot of fried food in my house. Normally I get to have a piece of fried chicken around the holidays or on a special occasion. Another thing you want to pay attention to is your sodium intake as well. You don't want to retain too much fluid. Too much sodium causes your heart to work harder. Although you don't wear your heart on your sleeves on the court you still want it to be in good shape.

Activity 2
You are what you eat.
Draw a picture of yourself using foods that you eat, and explain how you can develop better eating habits.

Respect

Respect is very big. You always give respect to get respect is what people always say but that's not always true. In some cases, you will give respect and still will not get the respect that you deserve from others, but don't ever let anyone change the person that you are striving to be. As a student-athlete, you may become popular among your peers and an individual that your peers look up too, so it is important to show respect to everyone in your school, from the principal to the custodians to your teachers to the kids that eat lunch at the table by themselves every day, your coaches, and the other coaches/team and the officials. A wise person once told me respect will take you to places in life that money cannot. Being young I've had to learn the hard way a couple of times lessons on respect. In school, once I got in trouble for being disrespectful. My parents pulled me from a very important playoff game that my team had. They still made me go and sit on the bench to support my team. I was forced to see the outcome of my decision and how it didn't just affect me, but my whole team. My coach begged my mother to let me play and she would not. She said to him "she is here to learn a lesson". I was so upset at her, but as I looked around at my teammates and coaches she did not let them down I did with the choice that I made. I am still in the process of learning how far respect can take me, but I have learned to humble myself. Proverbs 22:4 says "The reward for humility and fear of the Lord is riches and honor and life".

I learned that even some of your teammates may not like or respect you because of the person that you are. People don't need a reason not to like someone. Unfortunately, we are stuck seeing that in the world we live in every day. There is a lot of hate in the world, but there is also a lot of love. You have to remember that your successes may highlight other people's failures so never ask yourself or stress over why people may not respect or like you.

That is an issue that they have to deal with. Never make someone else's issues yours. In school, people may not respect you because of your good grades because they wished they had good grades. They may not respect you because of the bond that you have with certain faculty and staff members, and it's because they wish they had that bond with that person. They don't like you because you're the popular kid and they want to be popular. The list goes on and on. Don't let other people's opinions of you get to you. People are going to try to bully you, lie on you, start unnecessary drama, and all just because. Do your part by being a respectful student-athlete and let others deal with their own issues and insecurities.

Activity 3

Think of ways that you can show yourself, your coaches, your peers, and your teammates' respect.

In many sports, it takes a team to win so it is very important to build a bond with your team. To do this, everyone has to respect everyone including themselves. If a team can't get along then how are they supposed to play together? This includes opponents. Just because people say "never have mercy on the court", that doesn't mean to not have it off the court. Yea... you're playing against them and trying to beat them but when the game is over both teams should always have respect for each other.

Once I tried to walk off the court without shaking anyone's hand and my father let me have it and he made me go back and shake everyone's hand. He said to me they worked just as hard as you, actually better and you think it fair for you to just not only disrespect them but the game as a whole. That was a real eye-opener that day. My father is someone I have the utmost respect for, so to know that I disappointed him really got to me. He was right though, the other team really worked hard to beat us and they won fair and square.

I think back on that game I realize that they did earn my respect. Respecting your coaches is important as well because they want the same thing you want a win. Coaches, along with teachers see things in you that you may not see in yourself. Things that others may not see in you. If you piss a coach off too bad they don't care how good of a player you are, a bad attitude will have you sitting on the bench. Some people like to team hop. They get mad at their coach and teammates and go join another team.

Leaving a team does not solve all of your problems because coaches have their community and they talk to each other. That coach will give the other coach a heads up about you. The same thing in school you can be asked to be put into a different teacher's class, but I am pretty sure that she/he will have some of the same expectations that the other teacher had.

You don't want people to perceive your character as a disrespected student-athlete because then no one would want you on their team and you would have a bad reputation amongst teachers at your school.

Respect ties in with listening as well. When coaches are talking you should listen and do exactly as they say. You may not agree with them but if what they tell you doesn't work out then it on them, but if you turn around and do things your way then it's on you. One thing a coach dislikes is when they take their time to show you or tell you something that could help you and your team and you don't listen or do it right. No one likes a know it all. This makes the coach upset because they know what you're capable of and they can always see the better picture.

It's okay to be confident at what you are doing, but be humble. You also want to make sure that you show your teachers respect. Teachers work so hard to help young student-athletes achieve their goals. Teachers are on the front line of people that see your true potential and try to push you to achieve your goals. My absolute favorite teacher is my 6th-grade teacher from Salisbury Academy in Salisbury, NC. We did not always see eye to eye because at first, I thought she was picking on me, but after a long meeting, she explained to my mother and me that she knew what I was capable of in her class and she refused to accept less than my best. I thought to myself this teacher does care about me. My 7th-grade year my family moved to Okinawa, Japan, but I still keep in contact with her. Teachers, in my opinion, are so essential to one's success. You may have that one teacher that believes in you that you don't want to let down and another teacher that does not believe in you that you want to prove wrong. I am thankful every day for all of the teachers that I have had. They all have had a positive effect on my life in some type of way.

Grades

I have always had a passion for basketball ever since I was able to fully understand it. I don't know why basketball was the sport for me, I'm still figuring that part out. Ever since I was eight years old, I had a plan for my life. My plan has always been to continue my passion for basketball, get an athletic and academic scholarship to UNC, win a minimum of two championships there, get a degree, and get drafted to the WNBA. I also have a plan b if that doesn't work. My secondary plan is to study physics and get a job that will be suitable for me if basketball doesn't work out for me. It's important not to put all of your eggs in one basket.

Let's talk about the importance of education. I think Malcolm X said it best *"Education is the passport to the future, for tomorrow belongs to those who prepare for it today."*

School wasn't that hard when I was younger. Now it's different, I can say for many people that school life gets a little harder as you advance to the next grade.

You tend to get more homework, the work is more advanced, and teachers are trying to prepare you for the real world. Teachers don't have time to baby you. It is very important to keep your grade up. As a student-athlete, you have two important goals to perform well in the classroom and the game.

You won't even make it on the team if your grades aren't up to par. It doesn't matter how well you play you have to be in good academic standing to try-out for a team. Once you make the team it doesn't stop there, you still have to maintain good grades to play and to also get scholarships if you plan on furthering your education at a higher institute for learning.

You have to think about the fact that your skills are competing against other talented athletes' grades and your GPA is going against other people's GPA. You can never afford to slip or slack off on your grades because that can cost you a full ride somewhere. I try my hardest to make all "A's". Here and there I will make a couple of "B's", but my ultimate goal for myself is to be in the top five percent of my class. What good is it to have talent if I cannot show it off on a collegiate or professional platform, or worse a high school gym because of my grades?

What you do outside of school can have effects on your grades. Going through adolescence can be crucial and I don't think that parents understand that sometimes. They just want to call it puberty and want us to get over it. They always hit you with the line. I've been your age before but what they don't realize is that the world has changed and is forever changing. We are not growing up in the same era that our parents grew up in. People can be mean, especially those you call your peers.

As a young student-athlete you have the drama that's going on for no reason. You cannot allow yourself to get caught up in the drama. I learned this from experience. Everyone who says that they are your friend isn't always your friend. Choose your friends wisely because remember you become the company that you keep. Regardless, people sometimes judge you on the company that you keep. 7th grade was very difficult for me, I started with all A's and was playing basketball on a very advanced co-ed traveling team.

Things were going very well. The second quarter was good but classes started to get harder. I was still maintaining good grades like A s and B s while continuing to play basketball.

Third-quarter was the same as the second. Fourth-quarter was probably the hardest for me. Due dates got closer, the drama that I did not need to be involved with was getting out of hand, and basketball championships were going on. To solve the problem of my grades I took a couple of weeks off of basketball to focus on my academic life.

 I love the game of basketball, but I have a clear understanding that my education is my priority. Once I got things back in control that's when I got back to my favorite, basketball. The main reason grades are so important is because what if things fall through and I am not able to have my basketball career. What will I fall back on?

The way you are in your classes and your grades are a reflection of you.

Coaches want someone that completes their work on time, keeps good grades and stays on track. Student-athletes need to realize that the road in life you take might become a little bumpy, but eventually, it will smooth out, but ¼ of the bumps are caused by you. You have to push yourself beyond your breaking point. Get to the edge of the cliff and jump because someone will always be below to push you back up. Once you have become a student-athlete there are multiple roads you can take. For example, if you are becoming a successful student-athlete in high school, the first option is college. Most students look for top-ranked colleges that can help them get into the league. Another option is to play ball overseas.

Some people go overseas to make money for college or quick money. They also go overseas to have a different experience. Another option is the G League. The G League is a NBA minor league. One of my nicknames was D League. This league prepares athletes, coaches, and even staff for the NBA. In the G League players get paid around $7,000 per month or $35,000 in the five-month regular season. Thinking about my future all of these options sound good. I know for sure that I want to go to college.

It's a hard decision every player has to make, so it's important to make sure that you have people that have your best interest at heart talking in your ear. Some people believe college is a very important thing and I do too. An educated mind is a dangerous mind. I also believe that college is not for everyone. Going overseas could be good for some athletes, as well as joining the G League.

You have time to think about what you want to do, just figure out what will work for you and your future. I am about to start high school here in Okinawa, Japan. Often I think about playing overseas after I graduate, but I miss being in America and I know the value of furthering my education is very important so I think the college route will be better for me. After college, I may consider going back overseas if things don't work out with me in the WNBA. In my option female athletes get paid better overseas. Everyone has freedom of choice and everyone's decision is theirs to make, not anyone else's, and everyone should respect that when it comes down to others' careers. Good choice, bad choice, but always let it be your choice. When it's your turn to make your big decision after high school, you should feel confident about your decision, not scared, worried, or even sad. If you have any of those feelings then maybe you're not making the right choice. You should be comfortable because you should feel confident going into your next chapter of life whether it's: NBA, WNBA, G League, college, overseas,

or to a job.

Activity 5
What is your next move?
Write down a 4-year educational plan to get into your top 5 schools
Write down the pros and cons of possible career choices

Practice

Ever since I started playing basketball I have never been able to stop. I try to improve my skills by practicing different types of layups, jump shots and passes with my peers. I play with girls, boys, men, and women. Whoever is willing to get on the court with me, I will play them. Currently, in Japan, I play on an AAU traveling team called the Shooting. The first AAU team that I played within the states is called Team Fly. Whenever I'm in the states I try to link back up with them. I also play a lot of recreation basketball and sign up for different basketball events. As a teenager, it can be challenging at times to choose practices and games over hanging out with your friends, going to the movies, and different social events. My weekends are normally filled with games and tournaments, afterward would be the time that I would spend with my family. This was frustrating at first because every time my friends and I would make plans I would always have to cancel them due to obligations that I had with basketball. So with any sport that you plan on playing, ask yourself how dedicated do you plan to be because coaches don't care about a new movie coming out or about a birthday party, their job is to get you in shape for a great season. My coach asked me once do you want to be good or great? It is either hang out with friends all the time or work on your craft to help better yourself. I chose to continue building craft so eventually, it will help better my future. I feel like the decision I made was best for me because I still get to hang out with my friends from time to time and they also come to some of my games to support me. At the same time, I'm also setting myself up for success in the future.

If you have any problems that you are facing with prioritizing, just know that there is help available. If you trust these people enough you could go to your teachers, coaches, dad, mom, and even some close family members, or friends. Guidance is one of the things that we should seek as a young student-athlete.

For me whenever I have a problem or need help figuring something out, I usually call my dad for help. Even though I live with my mom and not my dad, it's easier for me to talk to him. I feel like he understands me better. When I talk, he listens to what I have to say, then he helps me come up with different solutions to the problem.

Another reason I go to my father more being that he is a private person just like me and we always see eye to eye on a lot of stuff. My mother is a bit of a firecracker, I am her baby girl so she is very protective of me and will go off without blinking an eye.

She is also hardcore and has the attitude that hey you just have to deal with it, and stop whining about it, "its call life". My mother and I don't always see eye to eye because sometimes she's not as compassionate as I would like for her to be, but I know she is that way because she wants me to know that the world doesn't hand anything to you on a silver platter. To get better at the game that you are playing you have to exercise for the sport. Sometimes you may have to do it alone or sometimes you may be able to do it with your friends or teammates. There will be plenty of days that you will not feel like practicing, but you have to push yourself. Also, you want to make sure that you are doing exercises that will help you and not hurt you. Don't push yourself too far, no your limits. You also want to make sure that you have on the right attire to practice. You should not have on a basketball shoe to practice soccer moves. You also want to make sure that you are staying hydrated while practicing. Make sure you eat at least 1 to 2 hours before you start practicing.

Activity 6

Make a conditioning schedule and make a list of all the things

Tips to help you on your journey to be a successful student-athlete If you have a passion for a sport and you want to get better then all you have to do is practice. You can practice any time you want and anyway. You need to be dedicated, stay focused, and know what you want to do. When I knew basketball was for me I was in the gym every day. For your future, you must strive for greatness.

I have already stated my tips to be a successful student-athlete but I will repeat them.

Tip #1 Keep God First and stay true to yourself and beliefs

Tip #2 Play all sports so that you know what's comfortable for you and something you can enjoy.

Tip#3 Build good chemistry with your teammates and make good friendships.

Tip#4 Make sure you put your education before sports because to be able to play you must maintain good grades.

Tip#5 Stay out of the drama and know who you are letting into your inner circle.

Tip#6   Make sure you are fully committed

Tip#7   Play the sport that makes you happy

Tip#8   Stay in shape.

Tip#9   Take classes that are going to set you up for your

future

Tip#10   Respect the game and everyone else involved in it

(including school administrator and teachers)

If you follow these tips and stay dedicated you are on the

right path to becoming an amazing student-athlete.

Activity 7
As you go through this journey ask people that you admire
(teachers, coaches, etc) what type of tips can they give you
on becoming a successful student-athlete

There are certain standard plays that you should know for basketball

Defense 2-3 zone

I believe was created by Coach Cam Henderson

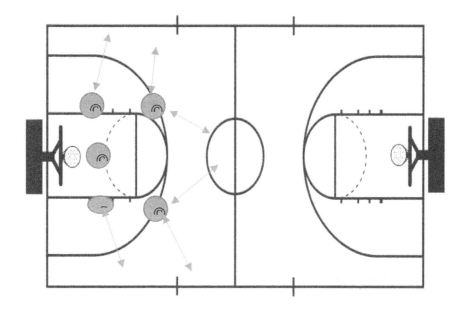

If you are a beginner in basketball the first zone defense you will learn is the 2-3 zone. This defense is the most simple and effective zone defense in my opinion. The 2-3 zone is used to protect the paint (free throw line in), and instead for jump shots around the perimeter.

The two players at the top are usually the point guard and shooting guard, then down low you have the center in the middle, and the small forward and power forward can choose either block.

Defense Play 3-2 zone

I believe to be created by Coach Bernard "Red" Sarachek

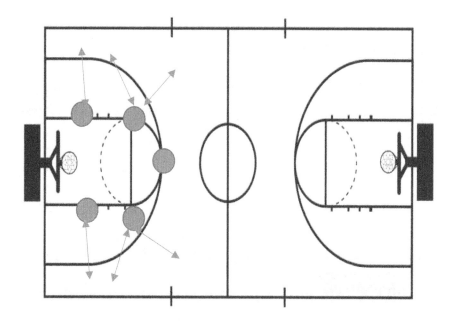

The 3-2 zone is another simple defense, it's basically the 2-3 defense but everything is reversed. You have your point guard, shooting guard, and small forward at the top, then your center and power forward on the two blocks. Just like 2-3 is used to prevent points in the paint, 3-2 is used to prevent points outside the paint and more around the perimeter like three-point shots or mid-range jump shots. It's recommended to use this zone defense against a sharpshooting team.

Defense Play 1-2-2′

I believe to be created by Coach Bernard "Red" Sarachek

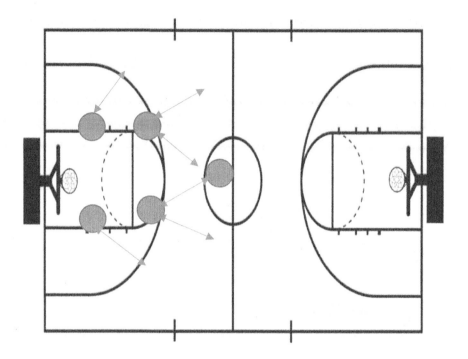

1-2-2 is a defense zone used to put pressure on the ball handler of the opponent's team if your coach or teammates realize that the ball handler is the one creating the opportunities to score or controlling their team 1-2-2 is the play to call. This defense gets the ball handler off their game and they tend to cause turnovers. For this play to work the player at the top has to be a really good, fast, and on point defensive player. The second-row players are there to help in case the first defense player gets beat if they do that person comes up to help and sticks with the ball handler until the next move is made. The back row with the bigs guards the basket so there aren't any easy buckets.

Offense Play - Pick and Roll

I believe to be created by Nat Holman and Barney Sedran

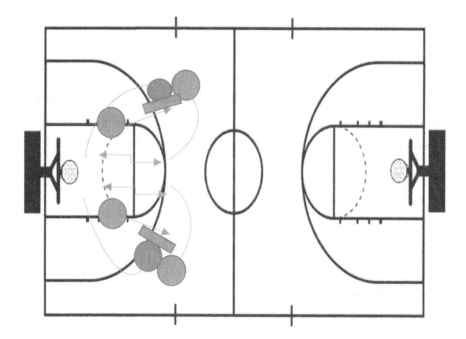

Pick and roll is generally run by a big and a guard. The big from the block runs up and plans their feet for a screen on the wing where the guard is. The set the screen on the defender's side that's closer to the middle of the court. Once the guard goes around the big open up and cuts towards the basket looking for a pass from the guard for an easy bucket. If the pass isn't there the guard could either drive, pass, or pull up for a jump shot.

Offense Play - Backdoor cut

I believe to be created by Franklin "Cappy" Cappon and Bernard "Red" Sarachek

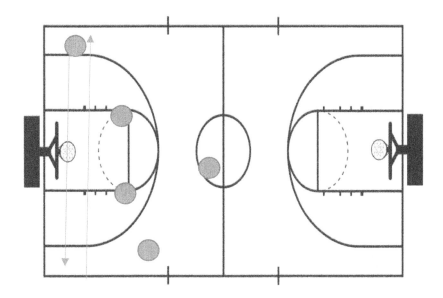

This plays used for either an easy drive to the basket or a corner 3-pointer. With this play I would recommend having a good shooter like a shooting guard running the baseline, all they have to do is go back and forth from each side of the baseline. Doing this will confuse the defender and they won't be able to keep up which allows the shooting guard or whoever is in that position to get open.

Offense Play - Stack

I believe to be created by Dr. James Gels

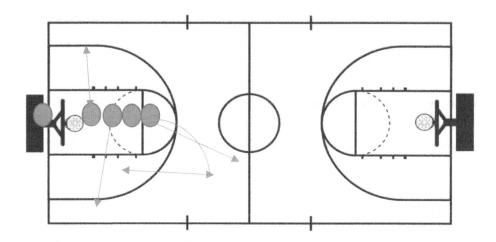

Stack for beginners is most likely the first set play you learn. A set play is a play that has certain moves that you have to follow. Saying this does not mean move like a robot doing the moves but know that flow and the way it's supposed to work, still play basketball.

Stack is very simple, you have everyone line up in a single file line at the out of bounds area. The order of the like is the center inbound the ball, first in line you have the point guard, and then you have your shooting guard, the small forward, and last the power forward.

You can always mix up the order and the places they go to. With this set up the power forward goes back to the free-throw line then drives towards the basket, the shooting and point guard flash out to the corners for threes, and the small forward flashes to the top of the key. The in bounders first choice is supposed to be the power forward that drives for the easy basket. If that pass isn't there they can pass to either of the guards for a 3-pointer. The last option is the small forward at the top of the key because of that where the ball is passed if none of the options are open and they need to reset the ball.

Know the game

In basketball, you have to know how to speak the basketball language. Listed below are a few terms that you should know by heart.

1. "Crash the Board"- When a shot is missed or being shot and you must go in for the rebound.

2. "Trap"- When there are two defensive players on one offensive player and the defensive players force a turnover.

3. "Help"- When a defender is beat on defense and needs their closest teammate to step up and help.

4. "Shot"- When a shot is in the air and everyone should be finding someone to box out.

5. "Cutter" - When an offensive player runs/cuts through the paint to get open.

6. "Baseline"-When an offensive player runs on the baseline side to side to get open.

7. "Outlet"- When a rebound is taken by the defensive and one of their teammates is already transitioning to the offense for a pass down the court.

8. "Ball"-When a player is open for the ball.

9. "Middle"- The same as a cutter, when someone runs through the pain to get open.

10. "Corner"- When a player is wide open in the corner.

11. "Swing"-Most likely the coach will tell their team to swing the ball to move the defense then find an open player.

12. "Screen/Pick"- When someone comes and plants their feet to block the defender from stopping their teammate from going around them to create a space.

13. "Switch"- When two players on defense come together with the players they are guarding and they swap the players they had been guarding.

14. "Motion"-An offensive play where players pass then cut and fill in the missing spots to get the defense confused and find an open player for an easy basket.

15. "Press"- When a team applies hard defense either at full or half court to force turnovers on the other team.

These are some basketball terms you will hear in a basketball career. They aren't hard to remember and they all help you win games. All these terms have helped me increase my skills in basketball including right now. They all play a big role in basketball.

Activity 8
Make a list of all the basketball terms you know and don't know, watch a video to show you how to do the basketball term and practice it.

My top five favorite female basketball players and why

1. Candace Parker- The reason Candace Parker is my number one favorite WNBA player is that I love the energy she brings on and off the court. When she's on the court she knows that its game time and she knows how to get focused. Off-court as well. She's always showing how much fun she and her daughter have and how she can be a fun person. Candace knows when it's time to focus and when it's time to have fun and relax. I love the balance that she has with her life.

2. Sky Digg- The reason Sky Digg is one of my favorite players is because of her accomplishments. Sky was an All-American for all four of her years at Notre Dame and always set school records for things like career points and steals. I want to one day break and set records.

3. Nneka Ogwumike-I like Nneka because she plays for my favorite team the Los Angeles Sparks, she was the

No.1 overall pick in the 2012 WNBA Draft, and she has an endorsement deal with my favorite brand, Nike. Our birthday is a day apart as well.

4. Tanisha Wright- Tanisha Wright helped the Seattle Storm win their second championship in 2010. The reason Tanisha Wright is one of my favorites is because she also played overseas in Israel, France, Poland, and Turkey. I think that is cool because I am technically playing overseas with my AAU team. We have traveled to places like Tokyo and Thailand for tournaments. A Lot of trips got canceled due to the recent pandemic, but I cannot wait to be able to travel again and compete against some of the best in the world. I have also considered playing ball overseas so I would love to have a conversation with her one day about her experiences.

5. Courtney Williams- The reason Courtney is one of my favorite players is because of her height, this might sound weird but I have my reasons. Courtney is 5'6

playing professional women's basketball. I am 13 and I'm already 5'7.5. No matter how much taller everyone was compared to Courtney she kept grinding and didn't let anyone stop her because they were bigger than her. She did not let her height determine her goals and future. If I don't grow anymore she gives me hope.

My Top five Favorite Men basketball players and why

1. Michael Jordan-People might think I like MJ because everyone else does and thinks he is the best but no. I sat down and watched *The Last Dance* a documentary about MJ and the Chicago Bulls and when I watched it made me realize how MJ and I had in common on the court. During practice he would always push his teammates to be better, in games everyone expected him to score every time the ball came in contact with his hands, and how he never let what anyone said get to his head. To him, the game

was not over until the last buzzer went off and that is how I feel. You can always make a comeback, whether it's the 1st or 4th quarter.

2. Kobe Bryant- I think Kobe is one of the all-time best because of his determination, even when he was hurt he never let that stop his strive, and if he missed a shot that wouldn't stop him from taking more. I am currently reading his book *Mamba Mentality. The* book gives you an insight into the type of person. I love the fact that he studies his opponents closely.

3. Dennis Rodman-Rodman is my number one rebounder of all time. I love how he knew exactly where to locate the ball and get his hands on it. His way of reading the ball on the court was outstanding and I want to be able to read and handle the ball just like him because believe it or not rebounding is a big part of basketball.

4. Lebron James-Lebron is one of my favorites because he doesn't let the media get to him. He does not fall

under peer-pressure. A Lot of people like to compare him to MJ and say he is the best but Lebron doesn't buy into it, he plays his game the way it was made for him to play. I love the fact that he went back to his city to bring them a championship. I love the fact that he stands by his word. I also admire all of the good things that he is doing for and in his community.

5. Kyrie Irving- Irving is another one of my favorites because of his ball handles and movement. He is not afraid to try anything on the court because he knows he can finish at the rim.

Activity 9
Make a list of your top ten players and write down the reasons they are your top ten

Perception

To be a student-athlete you need to have perception.
Perception of a sport means you have a good understanding.
Like I mentioned, don't play a sport just because your friend
plays that sport. Play a sport that you feel confident playing,
have a good understanding of, and most of all a sport that
you enjoy playing. Play for yourself and no one else. It
doesn't matter if your dad has 3 championship rings or if
your mother has a banner hanging up in her old high school
gym for a sport that she played 20 years ago. If your heart
isn't in the sport don't play it because in the end, you are the
one suffering when you could be enjoying yourself. You
live one life, so live it the way that is right for you.

Not all student-athletes go pro. Yes, you may be athletic and great at what they do but there will always be someone who plays harder, more dedicated, and even more athletic than you are. Everyone's goal should be to be that person that plays harder, is more dedicated, more studious, and more athletic.

In case you didn't know people are always watching you play your game on and off the court. Scouts are always out looking for new talent. Colleges have very high expectations for students that they want to recruit. They look for academic achievements, high GPA, and high course classes. Your GPA is very important because in college you will be traveling a lot so your coach wants to make sure that you can maintain good grades.

This is where the practice of being a great student-athlete plays its role. They want to know that you know how to work hard in school and on the court. If you can maintain good grades and talent in high school, then college won't be any different. Same thing with a different platform. The only thing that would need work is your self-discipline, independence, and time-management. Everyone knows that in college you could stay on campus or at home. Most students like to stay on campus because of the freedom of their parents. Most student-athletes are required to stay on campus. What some students don't understand is, living on campus has a lot of responsibilities.

You must make sure you wake up and be on time for your classes because in college you can't be late. Then you have to save up money for resources in your room like tissue, napkins, toothpaste, and food. Then you have to be on time for practices and conditioning. I'm pretty sure for sports there's more than one practice per day, which means your time for homework and practice has to be managed the right way. You also want to make sure that you have self-control. Knowing how to say no to things that you know could hinder your career goals. It's okay to say no to drugs, sex, and alcohol. You don't have to do what everyone else is doing to be cool. Besides, you have too much to lose.

As a student-athlete, you have to know how to be humble. People in interviews talk about being grateful for the opportunities they've been given but not all people realize how fortunate they are with the shots they have been given because a lot of people could be standing in your shoes but you were blessed enough to be in the position that you are in.

People's lives can change in the blink of an eye so never take anything for granted. Some students get scholarships and have a shot at making their dreams come true. There are a lot of stories about how some student-athletes come from poverty and made it. The reason why they make it in life is that they did what it took to make it and then some, not all student-athletes are rich or wealthy. Never feel like you have to have money to make it in life. Your life is what you make of it.

FUN

It's good for students to be able to stay focused on their goal but also have fun. Especially when you are young because you are only young once. When you take things too seriously it can lead to problems down the line. It's okay to laugh and smile and hang out with your friends. Never feel like there's no time for fun and the only thing that you have time for is the sport that you love. I agree to practice and conditioning is important because it improves your skills, but it's healthy to take time from your busy schedule and just relax and enjoy yourself. Having fun does not always have to include others. You may want to go and get a massage. Yes a massage, massages aren't just for adults kids can get them as well. Go to an amusement park, shop, or play your favorite video games in your room for a few hours. Sometimes you have to just get away from everything, school, and sport and just breathe. It's also important for student-athletes to maintain positive social media. Most teens have social media for example Instagram, Snapchat, and Twitter. As young-adults, we like to post without thinking. We post a lot of things to get more likes and followers without thinking things completely through. Student-athletes with social media must maintain a positive social platform and make sure that they don't post things that are offensive to others. Remember once you post something you can never take it back. You never want negative publicity. Remember a negative post can affect the future. If you are socially bullying someone you can be kicked off of a team in school and face severe consequences because of your actions. If you post-racial things on your social media platform you can face some serious backlash. You can lose scholarships, endorsements, be kicked out of school, and even worse lose your career. A student-athlete should never want that type of spotlight on them. You want to be known for your talent, good choices, community involvement, and devotion. I'm not saying the only thing you should post is yourself playing your sport. Let the works that you have done speak for you. Just be mindful of the post and imagine that you are posting and of the things that the people you are following are posting. Again just remembering once you hit post you can never take it back and that goes for emails and text messages as well.

Activity 10
Make a list of all the things that you like to do for fun when you're not focusing on your academics and athletics

Writing this book has changed a lot in me as a student-athlete. It's made me realize how much harder I should work to reach my goal. During this pandemic I've been running two miles two to three times a week, conditioning 4-5 times a week and workouts with some of the girls and boys that play basketball as well. I've really pushed myself hard this year because I know when I go to high school that everyone has high expectations for me and I don't want to give them doubt about my ability in the classroom and out on the basketball court. I know that I can be an amazing student-athlete and so can you. I've never had a bad problem with grades except for slipping up and dropping down to a C for the longest week of my life. I feel like I have matured in so many positive ways this year and have prepared myself well for high school. I hope while attending high school I will be able to jump every hurdle that comes my way. I'm not trying to rush life, I'm just trying to live it and enjoy it, especially basketball.

Make sure you follow me on the following social platforms

Instagram-@ballwdes   Twitter-@sheball_2

2017-2018   Salisbury Academy
MVP - Girls Varsity Basketball
Destiny Richardson

Psalms 46:5
God is within her, she will not fail.

Made in the USA
Monee, IL
28 October 2020